SILENCING SCIENCE

by **STEVEN MILLOY** and **MICHAEL GOUGH**

CATO INSTITUTE
Washington, D.C.

Library of Congress Cataloging-in-Publication Data

Milloy. Steven J.
  Silencing science / by Steven J. Milloy and
  Michael Gough.
      p. cm.
  ISBN 1-882577-72-8
  1. Research—Political aspects—United States.
  2. Research— Philosophy. I. Gough, Michael.
  II. Title.
  Q180.U5M495 1999
  303.48'3—dc21   98-48725
                                                        CIP

Printed in the United States of America.

CATO INSTITUTE
1000 Massachusetts Ave., N.W.
Washington, D.C. 20001

Contents

You can't pick up a newspaper or turn on television these days without somebody raving about something called the year 2000 crisis.

That's an election year, but they're not talking about Al Gore's charisma deficiency or the Republicans' problems in finding more charisma anywhere.

The year 2000 crisis (Y2K to Real Geeks) means your personal computer or mainframe computer may not be able to recognize dates or years after December 31, 1999. (Too much champagne on New Year's Eve and you might not either, but that's another story.) It's supposed to be a terrible problem that could interfere with everything from airline flights to Richard Simmons' TV ads (okay, so maybe it's not *all* bad).

But as we approach Millennium's End, maybe there are other things we should be worrying about. Why?

Because, in one sense, we're not really moving toward Y2K. We are heading backwards in time, in the wrong direction, toward the year 1000. Instead of 1999, next year will be 999. At least that's the way it seems sometimes.

Modern science has brought us previously unimaginable health, wealth, and knowledge. But as our world approaches the 21st century, forces more familiar to the Dark Ages than to the Computer Age are colluding to stifle science.

Science was last smothered on a large scale following the 5th century collapse of the Roman Empire when society plunged into a period of intellectual stagnation, ignorance, and poverty. Much like the World Wrestling Federation of today.

In the Dark Ages, state-of-the-art science meant alchemy, the "art" of trying to turn base metals into gold. Or astrology, the belief that the movements of the stars, planets, sun, and moon can foretell the course of human events.

For centuries, that's pretty much all the "science" that was available. It wasn't until the Scientific Revolution of the 16th and 17th centuries that scientific knowledge was again vigorously pursued.

Certainly modern society is not collapsing as the Roman Empire did. But we are slipping into a new form of darkness: one where it's popular, profitable, and politically expedient to suppress science.

How is this happening? That's what this little book is all about.

INTRODUCTION

Does science stand in your way? Do you know how to take advantage of things like ignorance, fear, and emotion? More important, do you *enjoy* taking advantage of them?

Maybe you're

- a personal injury lawyer whose multi-million-dollar contingency fees are threatened by scientific experts;

- an environmental extremist wondering why gloom-and-doom prophecies about manmade chemicals haven't panned out;

- part of the Food Police, whose crusade against "junk food" is being short-circuited by new fat and sugar substitutes;

- a government bureaucrat whose expensive new regulatory program is in danger of being exposed as unnecessary and wasteful;

- a purveyor of expensive waste treatment methods who sees economic opportunity in environmental hysteria;

- a promoter of a religion that declares knowledge is incompatible with religious faith;

- an ambitious man from, say, Tennessee, whose political future hinges on the public's belief that the Earth and its atmosphere resemble a backyard greenhouse, or

1

- a whacked-out technophobe trying to "eliminate" scientists, one by one, from your shack in the Montana wilderness.

If so, this book's for you. This is your handy-dandy guide to tried-and-true techniques to make just one thing certain: that science doesn't interfere with your own particular philosophy or world view, no matter how outdated, inaccurate, or just plain goofy that view may be.

In this book, you can learn

- How to stop scientific research before it can get started.

- How to keep scientific findings from spreading.

- How to bury existing science. Preempt debate. Harass and intimidate scientists. Make them wish they had chosen a safer occupation, something, say, like dance instructor on the *Titanic*.

You will also learn about surrogates for science such as *junk science*, *consensus science,* and the always-popular *precautionary principle* and its minions, *default assumptions.* They can make real science disappear faster than a Mafia accountant with a bag full of cash and, with a little guile on your part, the gulled public will never know.

After reading this book you'll know everything you need to help take society right back to ancient times—when solar eclipses were cause for alarm and the best available medical treatment involved "bleeding" and "balancing the humors."

So light a candle and put a fresh log in the old fireplace. Get out your quill pen and parchment for notes. Pour yourself a hearty cup o' mead and grab a crisp hunk of elk meat. The good old days are comin' back.

CHAPTER 1
Stopping Science

When possible, the best way to stop science is to prevent it from getting started. After all, the world can't miss what it never knew. (See *Presidency, Dukakis* and/or *Dole.*)

And it's a heckuva lot easier to keep the genie of science bottled up than it is to wrestle Mr. Science Genie back into that bottle once he's tasted a little fresh air.

To underscore the importance of preempting science, consider the following story about how the Inquisition racked up a big loss on its home court.

You say you want a revolution . . .

After studying ancient records, Polish astronomer Nicolaus Copernicus in 1543 published his theory that planet Earth revolves around our Sun.

The "Copernican system" contrasted simply and absolutely with the then-current "Ptolemaic system," which erroneously has Ol' Sol revolving around Earth.

Copernicus's theory was pretty much ignored for more than a century. Then it was confirmed by one Italian scientist, Galileo Galilei, using his new invention—the telescope. That spelled trouble for old Ptolemy.

Galileo published his Copernican corroboration in 1613. Trouble for Galileo was not far ahead.

Responding to criticisms of Galileo by both churchmen and astronomers, Pope Paul V ordered the

Inquisition to examine the Copernican system in 1616. The Inquisition pronounced the Copernican system "foolish and absurd," and Galileo was told not to believe in or teach it.

At first, Galileo obeyed. But in 1632, he published a book that compared the Ptolemaic and Copernican systems. The Inquisition, now under Pope Urban VIII, again called him on the carpet. Nearly 70, ill and traveling in a plague-filled winter, he journeyed to Rome.

This time, Galileo was tried and found guilty of teaching the forbidden Copernican system. He was forced to repudiate his beliefs and writings. A kindly archbishop was successful in getting Galileo's punishment commuted from "indefinite imprisonment" to house arrest, where he remained (without cable TV or the Internet) until his death in 1642.

Of course, Pope Paul V, Pope Urban VIII, and the boys down at the Inquisition had done too little, too late. They hadn't suppressed Galileo's writings completely. Eventually, the Copernican system, as confirmed by Galileo, became the foundation for modern astronomy and a cornerstone of the Scientific Revolution—perhaps the most serious challenge to faith until the Spice Girls' arrival.

Ironically, Copernicus was not a reclusive, out-of-control, religion-hating scientist. He was, in fact, a canon of the cathedral in Frauenberg, East Prussia. As such, he was completely under the authority and control of the Roman Catholic Church. Had the Church really squashed Copernicus's studies, what would Galileo have accomplished? What impact could his work have made on the Scientific Revolution?

So, when it comes to unwelcome scientific findings or advances, you definitely want to catch it before it's out of the test tube, so to speak. But how? Here are some basic techniques.

Surely that sounds draconian—but it's also effective. Consider the future of human cloning.

In February 1997, Scottish scientists announced the cloning of a sheep named "Dolly." Although sheep had been cloned before, previous cases involved genetic material taken from early embryonic cells. Dolly's genetic origin was a mature, specialized cell from a ewe's udder.

That clearly was a momentous advance for science.

As an embryo develops, its cells differentiate and take on special functions—e.g., becoming nerve cells, skin cells, or glandular cells. In carrying out their functions, specialized cells use (or "express") only the part of the organism's genetic material relevant to the cells' function.

What happens to the unexpressed genetic material? Is it somehow irreversibly modified or blocked so that it no longer can be expressed under any condition? Dolly's birth answered that question with a resounding "nay." (Or was it more like "Baa humbug"?)

This knowledge may lead to ways to produce cows that secrete medically important proteins into their milk. Or maybe methods to renew reproductive possibilities for people who have total germ cell (egg or sperm) failure. Or to methods of reprogramming human cells for the treatment of cancer, burns, or other disorders.

The Dolly experiment also set off a great debate about cloning humans. Many people question cloning on religious or ethical grounds. Others fear we'll end up with multiple clones of, say, Hitler or Martha Stewart.

But the sheep dip really hit the barnyard fan in January 1998 when physicist G. Richard Seed announced his intention to clone infertile people. Before you can say "Hello," Dolly and the ensuing debate prompted President Bill Clinton to reach for . . . the Big Ol' White House Panic Button.

While claiming to support areas of cloning research that could lead to medical breakthroughs, the president called on Congress to pass legislation banning research on the cloning of human beings. Then President Clinton's Food and Drug Administration police goose-stepped in to declare human cloning research would require FDA approval.

So much for human cloning research.

But shouldn't *some* research be outlawed anyway?

Of course. Science should never be the only consideration. We also have important social, religious, and ethical concerns and interests.

Some science is clearly reprehensible. Certainly the horrific experiments conducted by the Nazis on concentration camp prisoners or by the Imperial Japanese Army on World War II prisoners of war are utterly heinous and criminal.

Closer to home, the U.S. government also has behaved outrageously in the name of science.

For instance, a half-century ago the U.S. Public Health Service conducted experiments to see if syphilis affects whites differently than blacks. How? They simply withheld penicillin from black men infected with the disease. Indefensible.

Just after World War II, our government also conducted radiation experiments on humans. These trials may have been harmless, but they were undertaken without the informed consent of the subjects. Unjustifiable.

Ethics evolve, and it's true that there were no prohibitions against the syphilis and radiation experiments when they were done, but such things clearly are improper forms of scientific inquiry. By associating cloning with such horrific experiments, getting a ban on human cloning research will come about as fast—and easily—as a Michael Jordan slam-dunk.

But cloning really isn't comparable to those other cases. Cloning is simply the creation of an identical genetic twin. Mother Nature already can do it. Now we may learn to do it in a lab.

And who knows what medical or scientific advances might occur from simply trying? Remember, penicillin was discovered by accident. On a more mundane level, nonstick Teflon was only a byproduct of putting a man on the moon. Would life really be worth living or eggs worth frying without Teflon? (Besides, what would we call Teflon presidents like Ronald Reagan and Bill Clinton?)

Banning science education

Another way to short-circuit science is to prohibit its teaching. How? Just ape the "Scopes monkey trial," that's how!

After World War I, Americans started feeling a collective nostalgia for the relative simplicity and "normalcy" of prewar society. The war taught them that they really didn't care much for such technological marvels as machine guns or mustard gas.

In parts of the rural South and the Midwest, folks increasingly turned to religion for comfort and stability. Fundamentalist belief in the literal interpretation of the Bible soared in popularity.

Some fundamentalists saw Charles Darwin's theory of evolution—that organisms living today descended by gradual changes from ancestors unlike themselves and that natural selection determines which of the new organisms will survive and reproduce—as a threat.

They sought to eradicate Darwinism from modern society. They started, of course, at the schoolhouse.

During the early 1920s, a number of states passed laws prohibiting the teaching of evolution in public schools. Tennessee enacted its version of the laws in 1925.

Concerned about the laws' constitutionality, the American Civil Liberties Union volunteered to defend any teacher willing to challenge laws prohibiting the teaching of evolution. Young biology teacher John Scopes of Dayton, Tennessee, reluctantly accepted the challenge.

The renowned attorney Clarence Darrow, who defended Scopes, maintained evolution is consistent with the Bible. Still, did a jury find Scopes guilty? Does El Niño bring rain to California? *Yesssss!*

But while the anti-science crowd won the battle, they lost their war.

Although the Tennessee law stayed on the books until 1967, public outcry over the verdict discouraged other states from enacting similar legislation. Even Scopes' conviction was eventually overturned (on a technicality, but it was overturned).

Regulating science out of existence

Laws passed by legislators aren't the only governmental tools used against science. There are regulations imposed by panels of bureaucrats, too.

Should plants that can defend themselves against pests be regulated like chemical pesticides?

If you answered "yes," you're eligible to work at the Environmental Protection Agency (EPA) or for Monsanto Company. (If you wondered whether those plants could defend you against the telemarketer pests who call at dinnertime, you're probably not alone. Sorry. They can't.)

Most plants have some ability to resist pests and disease. Mechanisms of resistance include structural characteristics and toxic chemicals.

Advances in molecular biology have enabled scientists to exert more control in the breeding of plants. New genes for pest resistance to insects, mites, fungi, bacteria, viruses, and small animals can be introduced into plants.

Such technology is of great value to farmers, plant breeders, and geneticists, all of whom have been able to cross pest-resistant plants with others, producing high yields.

But good things don't last forever. Sometimes, with the government involved, they don't really get started.

In November 1994, EPA proposed to regulate what it called "novel pesticidal substances introduced into plants" along with the "genetic material necessary to produce them." The proposal was made under the existing law for pesticide regulation—the Federal Insecticide, Fungicide and Rodenticide Act or FIFRA—a law meant for chemical pesticides alone.

Under the new regulation, novel varieties of plants will be regulated like chemical pesticides.

Meanwhile, 11 major scientific societies, representing some 80,000 scientists, published a comprehensive report condemning the EPA proposal as scientifically indefensible. That didn't mean beans to the government.

The Monsanto Company didn't just support EPA's proposal. The company also pressured scientific societies to disavow their negative report. Why?

Despite allegations of worshiping laissez-faire capitalism, corporate giants like Monsanto realize they thrive under a rigid system of regulatory bureaucracy. They love those stringent regulatory requirements that are effective barriers to new competitors. They adore long delays and the red tape of government regulation that increase the cost of bringing new products to market.

While well-heeled companies like Monsanto (Motto: "We don't know what our name means, either") can bear such costs, smaller, entrepreneurial companies with shallow pockets are effectively locked out of the market.

And here's the anti-science angle. Because of new regulatory hurdles and high costs, smaller companies can't afford to do any more research work.

Henry I. Miller of the Hoover Institution said that this cynical strategy "makes losers of the research community, entrepreneurial biotechnology companies, and consumers." But corporate giants like Monsanto? They come out ahead.

Exactly how cynical is the strategy? In talking about the pest-resistant plants, a spokesman for Monsanto said, "A strong government oversight system is important to public confidence." This comes from the same company that has supported congressional efforts to pare back environmental, health, and safety regulation!

The federal funding squeeze

But suppose it is not possible to outlaw the objectionable science or to tie it up in loopy regulatory snarls. What next? Cut off the juice!

Money is to scientific research as electricity is to a light bulb. Turn the money on and light the lamp of knowledge. Turn off the juice, and we're back in the dark—which, of course, is where you want to be.

Fortunately for you (if not for science), the federal government provides about half the funding for scientific research in this country. This is especially true for basic scientific research—the type of rudimentary research that may or may not ever produce useful knowledge; if it does, it's usually only after years or even decades of work.

Getting a research program's federal funding canceled is easy. How easy? Sometimes it requires nothing more than a presidential executive order.

However you feel about the merits of fetal tissue research, the cutoff of federal funding for that research shows how it can be done.

Tissues taken from aborted fetuses (whether the abortions are spontaneous or induced) can be used to develop cell cultures and cell lines that are used in many areas of medical research.

Concerns about the reliability and safety of tissue from spontaneous abortions make tissue from induced abortions preferable. Researchers whose work may benefit from access to fetal cells are prevented, by law and for good reason, from getting involved in the timing, method, or procedures used to terminate pregnancies. They cannot offer inducements to mothers to terminate pregnancies.

Even though fetal tissue research does not lead to induced abortions, it uses tissues from such abortions, and, understandably, it's anathema to many people.

In 1988, President Ronald Reagan banned federal funding of fetal tissue research. This ban was maintained by his successor, George Bush.

Presidential orders banning federal funding cannot stop privately funded research—only legislation can do that. But the stigma associated with the prohibition on federal funding of fetal tissue research inhibited ALL researchers from looking at the possible uses of fetal cells.

The only real weakness of this method of cutting off funds is that a presidential executive order is only effective as long as the president wants it to be.

When Bill Clinton entered the White House in 1993, George Bush didn't leave town alone. Wife Barbara and the executive order against fetal tissue research, in effect, went with him.

Since then, scientists have reported promising results from fetal tissue research into the treatment of Parkinson's, Alzheimer's, and Huntington's diseases, spinal cord injuries, and diabetes.

See how political pressure produced the ban and lifted it? Do you have some ideas about what kinds of federally supported research should be stopped? THINK POLITICS.

The private funding squeeze

Of course, politics has its direct impact on scientific research that is government funded. Now what do you do about privately funded research that you don't like?

Can you spell S-T-I-G-M-A, boys and girls? That's the E-Z way to doom privately funded scientific research.

And keep in mind that your attack doesn't even have to make any sense.

Here's one of our favorites. A group of Harvard University researchers reported that biomedical scientists who receive private funding publish more papers, teach as much as their colleagues who have no private funding, and are equally active in academic affairs. But then they concluded that private funding adversely affects the academic productivity of researchers. Say what?

So go ahead and make that allegation. You'll be surprised how seriously people take you.

1. Taint the Research Because the Funder Is Evil
Few know the tobacco industry is a major funder of biomedical research. Since 1954, the tobacco industry has given more than 1,000 researchers almost $250 million. More than half of all U.S. medical schools receive research funding from the tobacco industry

But the tobacco industry is also controversial. Which is a little like saying Jack the Ripper was a bad date. The industry's hugely negative public perception has tainted its research funding—whether or not that research has anything to do with tobacco:

- A growing list of academic institutions bar researchers from accepting tobacco industry funding.

- The American Lung Association has announced that its journals no longer will consider papers funded by the tobacco industry for publication (talk about silencing scientists!).

- The *Journal of the American Medical Association* has editorialized that medical schools should refuse such money to avoid giving tobacco companies even a slim appearance of credibility.

- A subcommittee of the National Cancer Advisory Board recently recommended that the federal government no longer fund cancer centers accepting tobacco money. (Irony Alert! Harold Varmus, head of the National Institutes of Health, accepted tobacco industry funding for his research on oncogenes between 1984 and 1986.)

But this technique doesn't always work. Not everyone thinks that research is contaminated by the smell from its funding source.

The editors of the *British Medical Journal* criticized the policy of barring researchers from accepting tobacco industry money as misguided. It's a threat to medical science, to journalism, and, ultimately, to a free society, they said.

In a letter to *Science*, researchers from the American Red Cross argued that tobacco research funding is crucial to furthering biomedical research by allowing young investigators to start a research program and enabling established investigators to begin new projects.

Sidney Brenner is a researcher known for his trailblazing work on messenger RNA in the 1960s and later projects that popularized the nematode (a worm, for those of you who skipped biology that day) for genetics research. What does he say?

"There are very few people who will just give scientists money and say get on with it. The only condition is to do good work. Do good work. . . . My job is to do basic research. . . . I think that's a very important thing to do.... If we can create new science there, then it will be to the benefit of the whole of society and the future."

But don't be blinded by this smoke screen. Tainting the funder remains a solid, if unscrupulous, strategy to besmirch true scientific research. Don't be afraid to use it!

2. Profit above All Else
What if you can't sully the funder or the researchers? Well, maybe you can just let money do your talking.

In the 1970s, chemical manufacturer Du Pont had a dominant share of the worldwide market for chlorofluorocarbons (CFCs)—chemicals widely used as propellants in aerosol products.

A June 1974 report claimed that CFCs escaping into the atmosphere from consumer products could destroy the ozone in the stratosphere shielding Earth from the Sun's ultraviolet radiation. In short, we're all gonna fry—and soon.

Based on the report and the accompanying publicity, the public soon became concerned, if not hysterical, about CFCs.

In response to public concern, Du Pont bought a full-page ad in the *New York Times* (June 30, 1975) to say ". . . businesses can be destroyed before scientific facts are assembled and evaluated, and many might never recover, even though these facts may vindicate them. . . . If credible scientific data . . . show that any chlorofluorocarbons cannot be used without a threat to health, Du Pont will stop production of these compounds."

Although the use of CFCs in aerosol products was banned in 1978, CFCs were still used in automobile air conditioners, foam plastics production, and cleaning solvents.

The CFC controversy quieted down. That is, until 1985, when a "hole" was reported in the ozone layer over Antarctica.

Du Pont was faced with choosing between (1) conducting research about whether CFCs caused the ozone hole or (2) finding substitutes for CFCs. If you think Du Pont went with research, you've been standing too close to the warp coil again, Mr. Sulu.

The company went with Door No. 2. And it turned out to be the right choice—at least for Du Pont and its bottom line.

Du Pont holds patents on CFC substitutes called hydrochlorofluorocarbons (HCFCs). The HCFCs sell for several dollars per pound whereas CFCs sold for only about one dollar a pound. *Cha-ching!*

With (more expensive) substitute chemicals to sell, Du Pont became a big supporter of a 1987 international agreement to reduce or eliminate CFC use, an agreement known as the Montreal Protocol.

All in all, a business coup for Du Pont. But what about the scientific debate over CFCs and ozone depletion?

Science is not as far ahead as Du Pont.

The claim that stratospheric ozone is being destroyed by CFCs is based on an incomplete data record. Too little is known about past levels, current levels, or trends. While the Antarctic hole is a genuine phenomenon, its cause is likely something more complex than simply stratospheric CFC levels.

Du Pont started out wanting to use science to resolve the CFC-ozone depletion issue. But the company gave up arguing for science when a windfall business opportunity appeared.

No one can blame Du Pont for its business decision. But science certainly took it on the chin. But that, as they say, is the name of the game.

Intimidation and harassment I

Heavy-handed behavior seems to work for those whose career paths led them to become organized crime members, lawyers, or high school gym teachers. Why not you, too?

In 1994, researchers at the Mayo Clinic in Rochester, Minnesota, published a study on silicone breast implants in the *New England Journal of Medicine*. The study reported no link between silicone breast implants and connective tissue disorders.

Personal injury lawyers representing plaintiffs claiming harm from silicone breast implants were outraged. Not only did the study expose meritless lawsuits, but it also came at a crucial moment—in the same week as the deadline for plaintiffs to decide whether to accept a settlement from the manufacturers or to continue litigation.

For that mistake in timing, the Mayo Clinic researchers—and science—soon paid a heavy price.

The subjects in the Mayo Clinic's study were women living in Olmstead County, Minnesota, between 1964 and 1991. So plaintiff lawyers demanded access to the medical records of *all* women who lived in Olmstead County during that time, whether they were part of the study or not.

The Mayo Clinic provides most of the health care to the citizens of Olmstead County. Its Rochester Epidemiology Project (REP), built over a period of four decades, collects health information about all the county's residents and compiles histories of their medical care.

It is a unique national resource; nowhere else is there such complete health and medical information on a population. To date, the REP has produced about 1,000 publications analyzing dozens of diseases and medical conditions, and the National Institutes of Health ranked the 1995 proposal for continued funding of the REP in the top 1 percent of all the proposals it received.

But as a result of the demand for records, the Mayo Rochester Research Committee put a moratorium on additional studies about breast implants that use the Mayo epidemiology database. The moratorium is to last until the State of Minnesota passes protective legislation. As of June 1998, there is no such legislation and no such research. The lawyers' demands showed the way to shut down some epidemiologic research at the Mayo Clinic.

New England Journal of Medicine editor Marcia Angell noted that this had a chilling effect on all epidemiological research.

And that's our goal: put science in the deep freeze just like a 10-pound walleye.

Intimidation and harassment II

Another model of harassment took place at the University of Washington, where researchers were working on multiple chemical sensitivity.

During the past 15 years or so, a growing number of people have claimed to suffer from a variety of symptoms caused by low-level exposures to chemicals.

Their symptoms tend to be respiratory, neurologic, or systemic in nature. But they don't have well-defined physical or laboratory findings. The collection of symptoms—always growing, always shifting—has come to be known as "multiple chemical sensitivity" or MCS.

MCS advocates say chemicals damage the immune system—even a single exposure can be dangerous. But so far, no immunologic abnormality has been identified in those claiming to feel the MCS hammer.

A lack of scientific data to support the MCS theory has not stopped a burgeoning MCS industry—an industry with a real nose for contradictory science.

In July 1993, the prestigious *Annals of Internal Medicine* published a study about the role of immunologic, psychological, and neuropsychological factors in MCS. The five scientists who wrote the study concluded there was no link between any immunological abnormality and MCS.

They did, however, determine that "psychologic symptoms, although not necessarily etiologic, are a central component of chemical sensitivity." In particular, the five researchers found that MCS subjects had greater incidence of current anxiety and depression than did comparison subjects.

Big mistake.

In an April 1994 letter to the Office of Research Integrity of the U.S. Department of Health and Human Resources, an MCS activist accused the researchers of scientific misconduct.

The letter alleged the authors knowingly withheld critical information on the reliability and reproducibility of their research, something they knew (or should have known) would invalidate their conclusions.

The scientists also were accused of colluding with the author of an accompanying editorial on the paper. The author of the editorial was accused of promoting anti-MCS views as a paid defense medical expert on behalf of workers' compensation insurers, chemical companies, and others involved in chemical-injury-related lawsuits.

As a result of these mere accusations, the Office of Research Integrity recommended the University of Washington seize the records of the study's lead scientist. (Fortunately for endeavors to silence science, University of Washington officials understand that people accused by the Office of Research Integrity are "guilty until proved innocent.")

The allegations were investigated separately by the University of Washington's Office of Scholarly Integrity, the Group Health Center for Health Studies, the State of Washington Medical Disciplinary Board, and the federal Office of Research Integrity. In other words, just about everyone except Mulder and Scully from *The X-Files*.

None of the reviews, however, uncovered evidence of any misconduct.

Not happy with the outcome of the University of Washington inquiry, our persistent MCS activist appealed and forced another review by the University's Acting Vice Provost for Academic Affairs. Another complaint was filed with the Group Health Center, causing the Office of Research Integrity to get involved yet again.

The activist provides an additional lesson for all who want to silence science. He didn't limit his efforts to complaints about investigators. He went right after the unhappy researcher.

He organized pickets and threatened to "crash" a conference where the researcher was scheduled to speak. This threat required conference organizers to arrange for a plainclothes police officer and additional private security for the three days of the conference.

But, like practicing the piano, this kind of persistence eventually pays off. And it's a lesson for us all.

The researcher says the allegations caused him to run up bills and lose income. Not only that, he says, but the allegations also stopped his career progress.

"There is probably not a single MCS patient in the Northwest who will participate in any study or trial in which I was involved. Without a visible effort to counter the continued unfounded attacks against me and to restore my reputation, I have no future in the research or clinical trial treatment of MCS," he said.

For those of you scoring at home, it's now Harassment 2, Science 0. Game over.

Take away the tools

Under common law, creditors couldn't seize the tools of a craftsman who owed money because, without tools, how was the craftsman supposed to pay the debt?

But if you want to silence science, you are allowed to seize the researcher's tools. She won't be able to work, but don't worry about the science that won't get done. You don't want it anyway.

The animal rights movement shows you how.

Laboratory animals are indispensable to modern biomedical research. Scientists use them to test medical and surgical procedures, to study the biochemical mechanisms of new drugs, and to test new drugs for safety and efficacy before beginning human testing. Laboratory animal research has also led to treatments for sick animals.

It seems fair to call the animals "tools of research."

But the animal rights movement doesn't care about sick animals or new drugs. They're too busy trying to give animals the same moral value and rights as humans. They want to halt animal research. (Outside of Frankenstein movies, we don't do much laboratory research on humans; it's all on other animals. So if we get rid of animal research, we get rid of a big hunk of biomedical research.)

The People for the Ethical Treatment of Animals (a.k.a. PETA) show how to shut down animal research projects. The "Bion" program was a joint effort by the United States, France, and Russia to send monkeys into space as part of a study of the effects of weightlessness. PETA (1) flooded NASA and Congress with letters complaining about the program; (2) testified in congressional appropriation hearings against the program; (3) lobbied for a House bill killing Bion; (4) occupied the office of NASA administrator Daniel Goldin; (5) organized protests in France, Russia, Britain, Germany, the Netherlands, and the United States; (6) organized a celebrity letter-writing campaign to Congress; and (7) dressed up in monkey suits and rode bicycles around the U.S. Capitol for 24 hours. (Well, okay, we made up that last part.)

The campaign brought NASA to its Space Age, Tanglovin' knees. The agency withdrew from the Bion program.

PETA has also attacked the March of Dimes (*the March of Dimes*?) for spending nearly $1 million a year for research on birth defects. Members dressed as "bloody" cats carried a giant banner reading "March of Crimes: Stop Torturing Animals" in front of the March of Dimes headquarters. (That monkey suit idea wasn't so farfetched after all.)

And PETA is not only the dog in this fight. It's certainly not the most aggressive animal rights group at work today.

The Animal Liberation Front (or ALF) is classified by the FBI as a domestic terrorist group. Between 1986 and 1992, ALFists had a paw in as many as 14 different acts involving, arson, vandalism, and firebombing of research laboratories and laboratory animal breeding facilities. (Warning: We don't recommend these tactics. They are subject to criminal prosecution.)

PETA shows how a focused letter-writing campaign, congressional testimony, and protest demonstrations can stop the use of animals in biomedical research. Try those tactics. They may work in your own efforts to silence the science you dislike.

CHAPTER 2
Stopping the Flow of Scientific Information

W hat if you're too late? What if you didn't stop the science from getting done?

Don't panic. Just stop the flow of scientific information. It's easy to do.

Editing science

As the great left-hand-hitting philosopher Yogi Berra once said, "It ain't over 'til it's over."

Consider the report on global warming issued in 1996 by the United Nations Intergovernmental Panel on Climate Change (IPCC).

In 1995, the IPCC "approved" a draft report that was to be subject only to editorial changes. But subsequent changes went far beyond being merely "editorial." In other circles, this sort of thing is called a "complete rewrite."

Using their last at-bat, global warming aficionados stepped up to the plate and made deletions as well as a key substitution to eliminate the scientists' skepticism about their ability to associate surface temperature trends with human-caused greenhouse gas emissions.

Deleted sentences included the following:

• *While none of these studies has specifically considered the attribution issue, they often draw some attribution-related conclusions for which there is little justification.*

- *None of the studies cited [in the report] has shown clear evidence that we can attribute the observed changes to the specific cause of increases in greenhouse gases.*

- *No study to date has positively attributed all or part [of observed climate changes] to anthropogenic causes.*

- *Any claims of positive detection of significant climate change are likely to remain controversial until uncertainties in the total natural variability of the climate system are reduced.*

These sentences were replaced with

> *. . . the balance of evidence suggests a discernible [human] influence on climate.*

These and other changes were made after the report had been approved. They altered the content and the intent of the original report. Home run!

IPCC defended its actions by saying it was appropriate to modify the full report to match the more widely read *Summary for Policymakers*—an unusual approach given that, usually, a summary is made to match the report. Kinda like making the television program match *TV Guide*'s summary, isn't it?

In any event, based on this report, industrialized nations tentatively agreed to take steps to reduce greenhouse gas emissions.

All it took was a few clicks at a computer keyboard to delete uncertainty—a certain characteristic of science—from the IPCC report.

Deep-sixing science

Since the 1950s, radiation protection programs have

been based on two assumptions: first, even the smallest exposure to radiation can cause harm; and second, the risk of harm increases linearly with increasing radiation dose. Together, these assumptions are known as the linear no-threshold theory (or "LNT" for acronym lovers).

The consequences of LNT are both many and wide-ranging: Doctors tell women that mammograms increase cancer risk. EPA scares homeowners by saying that radon gas in the home can cause lung cancer. Hundreds of billions of dollars will be spent over-cleaning former nuclear weapons facilities. The promise of safe, cheap, and clean electricity from nuclear power plants faded faster than flavor from bubblegum.

Meanwhile, an enormous and powerful radiation protection industry has emerged. Members include federal and state regulators, government-funded researchers, and symbiotic commercial enterprises such as those in the radon testing and abatement businesses.

The radiation protection industry has managed to bulldoze any science that contradicts the LNT theory, the cornerstone of its power.

In 1991, the Johns Hopkins University completed a U. S. Department of Energy-sponsored $10 million study of 700,000 nuclear shipyard workers.

The data in that study, which has been described as the largest, best-conducted study on cancer risk from occupational radiation exposures, failed to reveal any risk associated with radiation exposure.

Despite that startling result—or because of it—the study never (so far, at least) has seen the light of day. It was never published in the scientific literature— very unusual for a study hailed as the largest and best of its kind. The only notice of the study was a brief one-page summary in an obscure DOE publication— *Health Bulletin* 91-3 (September 1991).

As a result, hardly anyone knows about the study. And the radiation protection community wants to keep it that way.

When the principal investigator was asked if there were any plan to publish the study in the open scientific literature, she suggested taking that inquiry to the Energy Department.

But that only prompted three excuses for no publication in the open literature: (1) the principal researcher might be redoing the analysis; (2) she ran out of funds to write up the results; and (3) she hadn't had time to write up the results.

Their next response was going to be "My dog ate the data."

In any event, it's hard for science to make headway when no one knows it ever took place.

Contract on science

In 1990, University of California at San Francisco researchers completed a study comparing drugs used to treat hypothyroidism. The study was funded by Boots Pharmaceuticals, Inc., the then-dominant force in the $600-million-a-year market for hypothyroidism medication.

After testing Boots' Synthroid against a rival brand called Levoxyl and two generic brands, researchers concluded the four drugs were essentially equivalent.

When the results were shared with Boots, the company tried to discredit the planning, execution, and data collection of the study. But two investigations by the university revealed only minor and easily correctable errors.

In April 1994, the study was submitted for publication to the *Journal of the American Medical Association.* Aware of the controversy, *JAMA* had the paper reviewed by five experts. Passing review, the study was accepted for publication in November 1994 and scheduled for publication in January 1995.

But less than two weeks before the study was to be published, the researchers notified *JAMA* they wanted to withdraw the paper from publication because of impending legal action by Boots. It turned out that the original research contract contained a provision prohibiting publication without the company's written consent.

Because Boots had not granted permission, the study could not be published. It was almost the perfect crime But, in this case, the paper did not die.

On April 25, 1996, *The Wall Street Journal* published a front-page article detailing the study's unhappy fate. After the ensuing media storm and pressure from the Food and Drug Administration, Knoll Pharmaceuticals, which bought Boots in 1995, agreed to let *JAMA* publish the paper. In April 1997, almost seven years after the research was completed, the study was published in *JAMA*

Close, but no cigar.

Playing the lawsuit card

In October 1983, the New York Public Interest Group (NYPIRG) released a study called "What's Blowing in the Wind?" As reported by the Associated Press, the study warned of health risks supposedly associated with a Brooklyn landfill.

In February 1987, scientists from Brooklyn College submitted a manuscript analyzing the NYPIRG report to the journal *Northeastern Environmental Science.*

They criticized the NYPIRG report on a number of points: "loaded" survey questions, poor survey response rate, dependence on a number of unvalidated assumptions, unconsidered confounding risk factors, a failure to test for statistical significance, selective reporting of results, and no independent peer review, to name a few deficiencies. There hasn't been that much criticism in Brooklyn since the Dodgers moved west!

The Brooklyn College scientists concluded the report's link between health effects and the landfill was arbitrary and without scientific justification. In other words, nothing but garbage.

After receiving the scientists' critical manuscript, the *Journal* submitted it to NYPIRG and several independent reviewers for evaluation before any decision to publish it. NYPIRG agreed to review the manuscript but never submitted its evaluation.

Instead, NYPIRG officials denounced one of the authors and threatened libel actions. The editorial staff regarded the threat of libel seriously enough to discuss the matter with the directors of the *Journal*.

Unswayed by the threat, the *Journal* went ahead and published the critique. NYPIRG never followed through on its threat, however.

Now, don't let that persuade you that threatening a libel lawsuit is a bad tactic for silencing science. Just beware of the major weakness—under our law, truth is a defense against libel. In other words, saying Roseanne is a bad actress may not be libelous.

Impeding criticism

Let's say you base your career on "junk science." The last thing you need is critics. So what do you do? As the great humanitarian Al Capone might say, you could always silence 'em.

In 1979, University of Pittsburgh researcher Herbert Needleman reported that exposures to low levels of lead cause lower IQs and delinquent behavior in children. The study catapulted Needleman into national prominence faster than you can say "lead paint."

But some scientists expressed concern about the study because an exceptionally large number of study subjects were inexplicably dropped from the analysis. And the study's methods were not described sufficiently for other scientists to understand them.

Even EPA was skeptical. During 1982–1983, when EPA considered revising the air quality standards for lead, an EPA review panel concluded the study neither supported nor refuted the hypothesis that exposures to low or moderate levels of lead were associated with cognitive or other behavioral impairments in children.

In 1990, scientists Claire Ernhardt and Sandra Scarr were independently retained by a defendant in a Superfund case involving lead exposures. Needleman was hired by the Justice Department, which was acting on behalf of EPA in the same case. Because Needleman would be relying on his own data, the court approved the defendants' request to let their experts examine his data.

When Ernhardt and Scarr visited Needleman's office to review the data, he refused them access to his raw data or to a codebook for computer printouts. And he refused to provide an explanation for cryptic remarks on the computer printouts, despite the court order. Nice host, huh?

Scarr and Ernhardt were not even allowed to make photocopies. Instead, to substantiate their observations, they had to copy, by hand, pages and pages of data. The Justice attorney present at the time asked

Ernhardt and Scarr not to discuss their findings outside the case being tried. Ernhardt and Scarr refused the request and left the premises.

Shortly before the case was settled in November 1990, the Justice Department, at Needleman's behest, again sought to have Ernhardt and Scarr return or destroy their notes and report. Ernhardt and Scarr found a lawyer for the ensuing litigation over the notes.

In his April 1991 decision in Ernhardt and Scarr's favor in *U.S. v. Sharon Steel,* the judge wrote, "The pursuit of scientific knowledge is, in theory, an open process. There is something inherently distasteful and unseemly in secreting either the fruits or seeds of scientific endeavors. . . . The only harm or prejudice asserted by Dr. Needleman appears to be the risk of academic criticism. . . . This is insufficient justification for the relief sought by plaintiff."

But maybe you'll get lucky. Maybe you won't run into critics who are so persistent. And maybe your case won't be heard by a judge who knows what science is about.

The Oliver North method

Remember how Col. Oliver North got rid of evidence in the Iran-Contra affair? It can work for you, too. Invest in a good shredder—just like the one used by the California Environmental Protection Agency (Cal-EPA).

In April 1996, Cal-EPA scientists were ordered to destroy research data and internal documents that differed from their administrator's final decisions. And Cal-EPA was clever about it. They called it a "records retention" policy. And Watergate was just a constitutional protection operation.

According to Cal-EPA officials, this "policy" was intended to protect the confidentiality of sensitive internal debate over research and foster free exchange of opinion by protecting the identity and views of the scientists involved.

Huh? They were going to foster free exchange of opinion by obliterating all evidence of it?

But the policy was short-lived. It was roundly criticized by scientists, environmental groups, and free-speech advocates who claimed the policy was designed to do just the opposite—censor debate on public health risks.

In October 1996, Gov. Pete Wilson ordered Cal EPA not to destroy records. Cal-EPA said that instead of destroying records, it would maintain them in confidential files—in other words, we won't shred the documents, we just won't tell you where they are.

Hiding data

Sometimes scientific debate can be squelched simply by making sure there's nothing to talk about.

In November 1996, EPA proposed stringent air pollution standards that the agency claimed, among other things, would save 20,000 lives a year. That particular estimate was based on two epidemiologic studies: a 1993 study led by Harvard University researchers (the "Six-City" study), and a 1995 study led by C. Arden Pope of Brigham Young University (the "Pope" study).

As the sole basis for the estimate of lives to be saved annually, the Pope and Six-City studies naturally attracted attention. With good reason.

The Pope study reported a 17 percent increase in mortality for people living in the most polluted areas versus those living in the least polluted areas. The Six-City study reported a 26 percent increase in mortality for people who live in the most polluted areas versus the least polluted areas.

But the claims seemed shaky. As a rule of thumb, epidemiologic studies of the type relied upon by EPA are too imprecise to reliably identify increases in risk of 100 percent or less.

The Pope and Six-City studies never measured any individual's exposure to air pollution and did not rule out competing risk factors that could have accounted for the reported increases in mortality.

Accordingly, Congress requested that EPA and the studies' authors make the underlying data available for independent review.

Such data sharing is customary practice among scientists, but it was a foreign concept to the study authors, who refused to provide the data. And EPA backed them up!

The agency said that many of the data in question are proprietary and protected under various agreements that the researchers made. The Harvard scientists whined that giving up the data would completely cripple their ability to go out and do epidemiologic studies of any type.

But the public furor over this issue forced EPA to back down and to work out a pseudo-compromise. The researchers agreed to share the data with the Health Effects Institute (HEI), a research institute half-funded by the EPA and half-funded by the automobile industry. HEI expects to complete its review in two years, by 2000, if all goes well.

Of course, before then, the new regulations will be in effect. Not only will the HEI review come after the fact, the agreement between Harvard and HEI is based on a condition that HEI not share the data with other organizations or individuals.

That's data sharing—NOT!

More intimidation and harassment

Earlier we said that it is possible to intimidate and harass scientists into not conducting science. The same tactic works to keep science from spreading.

In the case of silicone breast implants, the plaintiff attorneys harassed researchers who disagreed with them in court and interfered with their relationships with their employing institutions through legal attacks and media assaults.

As a result they made it much more burdensome for researchers to testify in court. This has diminished the usefulness of science in dealing with difficult issues such as whether breast implants cause harm.

An Associated Press wire story about Dr. Peter Schur started an 11-month investigation of Schur by Brigham and Women's Hospital. The story reported that Schur had conflicting roles: one as editor of the medical journal *Arthritis and Rheumatism* and another as a $300-an-hour consultant and expert defense witness in silicone breast implant trials. While editor of *Arthritis and Rheumatism*, Dr. Schur published his own article defending implants' safety and worked on two major studies about their possible health effects.

A three-member Brigham and Women's committee concluded that Schur had not violated any explicit hospital policy and it found no evidence of biased research. Remarkably, however, the investigation resulted in the imposition of new restrictions on the hospital's scientists.

Now, physicians who want to serve as expert witnesses or paid advisors to attorneys must ask permission from their department chiefs.

Academics and bioethicists expect that the restrictions will mean researchers, afraid that the very process of approval will open them to scrutiny and conflict of interest charges, will be increasingly reluctant to serve as expert witnesses.

That helps lawyers distort the public's understanding of science since the researchers are the most credible spokespersons on the conclusions and implications of their studies.

But even without such restrictions, the threat of legal harassment has affected researchers. Dr. Charles Hennekens, an epidemiologist and chief of preventive medicine at Brigham and Women's Hospital, offered two of his top assistants what would normally be the highly coveted first authorship of an important study of silicone breast implants. They both turned him down. Evidently, they did not want to contend with the attacks that might be heaped on them and their research by the plaintiffs' bar or the potential hassles if their research was dragged into courtrooms.

Can you think of a more effective way to silence science than to convince scientists not to speak up about their own work?

Discrediting viewpoints

Some scientific findings or viewpoints can be attacked or questioned based on nothing other than their source.

When studies from Harvard University and Mayo Clinic failed to link silicone breast implants with immune system disorders, implant activists took aim at the two institutions, not the methods or findings of the researchers.

A co-chairman of Command Trust Network, the silicone breast implant activist group, said this on the television program *Frontline* (February 26, 1996):

"First let's get over the myth that just because Harvard or the Mayo Clinic or Yale says something that it's correct. We know where the bread is buttered. We know who gives the funding. Manufacturers fund, scientists do their studies."

Plaintiff lawyers in the silicone breast implant litigation attacked the *New England Journal of Medicine*, implying that it had been paid by the manufacturers of silicone breast implants.

Put on the defensive by these allegations, Dr. Marcia Angell, executive editor of the *Journal*, replied: "That's not at all credible. . . . Harvard and the Mayo Clinic are great institutions. The *New England Journal of Medicine* is a great institution. We would be crazy to allow ourselves to be bought by a company."

Perhaps, but this controversy made the *Journal* more sensitive to criticism that sources of funding might bias scientists' reporting of results.

In September 1996, the *Journal* published a study reporting that the diet drug Redux increased the risk of pulmonary hypertension, a life-threatening lung condition.

But an accompanying critical editorial by Dr. JoAnn E. Manson of Harvard University and Dr. Gerald A. Faich of the University of Pennsylvania said the increased risk may not even exist at all. At the very least, they said, the benefits of using Redux outweighed its risks.

About one month after the study and editorial were published, the *Journal*'s editors strongly rebuked Manson and Faich for failing to disclose they had been paid consultants to Redux's manufacturer and distributors. (The rebuke didn't mention that Manson and Faich had complied with the *Journal's* usual request for information about potential conflicts of interest.)

Then in December 1997 the editors turned on Jerry H. Berke, the author of a book review that appeared in the *Journal*.

The book in question claimed that chemicals in the environment are responsible for an epidemic of cancer. Book reviewer Berke criticized the book's lack of science supporting these claims. But he was also the medical director for a large industrial company.

According to *Journal* editor Jerome Kassirer as reported in the *Washington Post* (December 28, 1997), "It's laughable that Berke would think he could write an objective review of the book given that he was an employee of W. R. Grace."

We guess the editors must have forgotten what they said when they were attacked by the silicone breast implant lawyers: "We would be crazy to allow ourselves to be bought by a company. . . ."

Sure, they would have to be crazy to, but you don't have to refrain from suggesting they're on the take. Just be careful that your smear attempt doesn't backfire.

On February 24, 1994, Ted Koppel's ABC News program *Nightline* aired a piece on global climate change. According to Koppel, the story was the direct result of a suggestion from Vice President Gore that *Nightline* look into "some of the forces, political and economic, behind what he would regard as the anti-environmental movement. . . . The vice president suggested that we might want to look into connections between scientists who scoff at the so-called greenhouse effect and the coal industry, for example."

But in closing the piece, Koppel said, "There is some irony in the fact that Vice President Gore, one of the most scientifically literate men to sit in the White House . . . is resorting to political means to achieve what should ultimately be resolved on a purely scientific basis. . . . The issues have to be debated and settled on scientific grounds, not politics. . . . The measure of good science is neither the politics of the scientists nor the people with whom the scientist associates. It is the immersion of hypothesis into the acid of truth."

But Koppel and other reporters like him can't cover every story. They're not likely to catch you if you discredit a scientist or his views that you dislike. At least, it's worth a try.

Blackmail

In November 1994, EPA proposed new air pollution standards for sulfur dioxide. In the proposal, EPA requested comments from asthma specialists about the medical significance of the reported effects in asthmatics exposed to sulfur dioxide.

The mining industry asked four asthma specialists to review the relevant studies and EPA staff documents. The experts included Dr. Alan Leff, a professor at the University of Chicago, and Dr. James Fish, a professor at the Jefferson Medical College in Philadelphia. Both are well-known experts.

After reviewing the relevant documents, the experts concluded that the proposal was not justified by the available science. They prepared written statements of their conclusions for submission to EPA.

Dr. Leff agreed to testify at a public hearing. Dr. Fish agreed to have his statement presented at the hearing.

On February 2, 1995, however, Dr. Leff informed the mining industry that the American Lung Association (ALA) and its medical arm, the American Thoracic Society (ATS), advised him not to attend the hearing or present a written statement.

The ALA said his participation in the hearing would compromise his prestigious position (with honorarium) as editor of the *American Journal of Respiratory and Critical Care Medicine*, an ALA journal.

So Dr. Leff backed out of the hearing and asked that his written statement not be submitted. Dr. Leff later asked the ALA if he could attend the hearing and present a personal statement rather than a statement on behalf of the mining industry. This request was refused as well.

The ALA also advised Dr. Fish, who chaired an ATS committee, not to submit his written comments.

Their scientific work had already earned Dr. Leff and Dr. Fish prestigious positions in the ALA as well as respect in the wider scientific community, but ALA officials evidently decided it was not fit for public presentation. We don't know why.

The EPA was pleased enough with ALA to award its Washington office $3.7 million in the early 1990s. The ALA's silencing of two scientists may have pleased EPA because it eliminated two voices that opposed the agency's proposed regulations.

In any event, the opinions of Drs. Leff and Fish were not heard. Maybe you'll be able to find a public interest group that will accept a little of your money. Maybe it will find itself in a position to spread a message you like or quash one you don't.

The power of the press is legendary. But there's a lot more to that power than just reaching large numbers of people. Consider this snippet from the saga of the pesticide DDT.

In her 1962 book, *Silent Spring*, Rachel Carson made a lot of noise about manmade chemicals, especially DDT. In particular, she claimed that DDT had brought birds such as the robin and the bald eagle to the brink of extinction.

But in September 1963, Dr. Thomas H. Jukes, a biochemist at the University of California, published an article in the *American Scientist* contradicting Carson's claims. Relying on bird counts from Audubon Society publications, Jukes noted that, since DDT use had become widespread, the number of robins observed had significantly increased.

Jukes commented that "the increase is presumably significant, and the robin does not appear to be on the verge of extinction." The bald eagle wasn't dying out either, Jukes found. Despite 15 years of heavy and widespread usage of DDT, Audubon ornithologists counted 25 percent more bald eagles per observer in 1960 than during the pre-DDT 1941 bird census.

Using those bird counts, Jukes and other distinguished scientists maintained birds in North America were thriving despite the widespread use of the Carson-condemned DDT.

By the 1970s, however, the Carson-inspired environmental movement was in full bloom, the newly created EPA was looking for regulatory targets, and DDT was on the chopping block. In the April 1972 edition of *American Birds*, a magazine published by the National Audubon Society, editor Robert S. Arbib, Jr., accused "certain paid 'scientist-spokesmen'" of lying about the bird counts on behalf of the pesticide industry.

On August 14, 1972, the *New York Times* recounted Arbib's accusations in a story titled "Pesticide Spokesmen Accused of Lying on Higher Bird Count." And at the urging of the *Times* reporter, Arbib named five scientists in the article.

Three of the named scientists filed a $12 million libel suit against the *Times* and the National Audubon Society.

During pre-trial depositions, Victor Yannacone, a founder of the Environmental Defense Fund (EDF, a spin-off of the National Audubon Society) said that discussions had been held at the EDF with the vice president and other associates of the National Audubon Society. Those talks centered around ways to silence or discredit opponents of their stand on DDT.

In July 1976, a jury decided that the National Audubon Society was not guilty. But it found the *Times* liable and awarded the three scientists $61,000. The jury found that the article's statements were clearly libelous and made with "malice"—i.e., knowing the charge was false or made with reckless disregard of whether it was false or not.

The *New York Times* appealed the verdict. On May 25, 1977, Judge Irving Kaufman overturned the jury verdict on the grounds that the *Times* was justified in reporting the charges because they were "news-worthy." Regardless of whether they were false.

Judge Kaufman ruled that, "What is newsworthy about such accusations is that they were made. We do not believe that the press may be required under the First Amendment to suppress newsworthy statements merely because it has serious doubts regarding the truth. Nor must the press take up cudgels against dubious charges in order to publish them without fear of liability for defamation. . . . The public interest in being fully informed about controversies that often rage around sensitive issues demands that the press be afforded the freedom to report such charges without assuming responsibility for them."

So the National Audubon Society provides you a lesson on silencing science. Discredit a scientist by misrepresentation, but don't spread the word yourself. Get the news media to do it. Their legal protection is your shield, too.

The media sales job

Instead of engaging in scientific or political debate, some in the anti-science mob have opted to work on the news media.

Consider the advice to members of the Union of Concerned Scientists (UCS) for addressing the global warming issue with the media:

> *1. **Stay on message.** The SSI [Sound Science Initiative] message is simple: (a) Global warming is a serious problem. (b) It will have serious impacts on human health and the environment. (c) We must take action now to fight global warming.*

> *2. **Don't confuse them with doubt.** In other words, don't talk like a scientist, with caveats and error bars. Emphasize the word "consensus."*

> *3. **Don't talk too much.** A Dan Rather sound-bite is about 7 seconds. You may get 15–20 seconds on local shows, or the equivalent of three or four sentences in print. So practice your sound bites, and don't get trapped*

into giving the reporter what he is looking for. Set your time limit for interviews in advance, at 15 to 20 minutes so that you can terminate the interview before you are in over your head without appearing to be evasive. . . . Your main purpose is to advocate, not to educate.

What this union of scientists is concerned about is anyone's guess; it's certainly not science.

CHAPTER 3
Filling the Void When Science Is Silenced

So you've silenced science. Congratulations. But your job is not quite finished.

In the absence of science, there's a void to fill. If you don't fill it, someone might notice that real science is missing and do something.

So you must fill the vacuum with "anti-science"—official science, consensus science, junk science, or the precautionary principle.

From watching your opponents' exertions, you know that science can be hard work. You want to avoid that, and anti-science is the ticket. It does not seek to learn the truth. Instead, it simply declares, concocts, or assumes what the truth is.

Official science I

Official science requires that some "authoritative" body declare what the state of science is. Official science during the Inquisition said the Sun revolved around Earth.

How can you get official science established? Consider the mammogram controversy.

In February 1997, a National Institutes of Health (NIH) panel concluded that the costs of widespread mammographic screening for women in their 40s outweighed the benefits.

The costs included testing thousands of women, few of whom would have breast cancer. Moreover, many women without cancer would have "false positive" results that would require retesting and in some cases exploratory surgery.

No one sought to deny mammograms to any woman, and everyone agrees that women at high risk should have them. The NIH panel simply decided against recommending widespread screening because of the anguish and expense from false positives.

But the conclusion outraged the breast cancer advocacy groups that were already convinced of the value of mammography. The breast cancer lobby, in turn, convinced members of Congress to blast the report.

The Senate called in the chairman of the NIH panel to defend the panel actions. Then, in a nonbinding resolution, the Senate voted 98 to 0 to support mammograms for women in their 40s. One senator even threatened the funding of the National Cancer Institute, and, reportedly, the job of its director.

Two months later, another panel, this one assembled by the National Cancer Institute, issued a far different report. It concluded that the benefits of mammography outweigh the costs for women in their 40s. But it offered no new data to account for the different conclusion.

The second report, publicly endorsed by the Secretary of Health and Human Services, the president, and several senators, didn't settle the real science. But it did settle the "official" science.

There's an important lesson here. Political decisions can override science.

You can be sure that with the passage of time, the endorsement of widespread mammography screening will be referred to as a scientific decision. You can bet that the scientist who doubts the value of widespread mammographic screening will think carefully before taking on official science.

Official science II

One legacy of the Gulf War is a legion of veterans who complain of something eventually called Gulf War syndrome. The syndrome, similar in many ways to multiple chemical sensitivity, has no known causes or unifying symptoms.

Exposures to trace levels of nerve gas (if they occurred), exposures to heavy smoke from oil well fire, exposures to kerosene from space heaters, and exposures to insecticides have all been suggested as causes.

Symptoms range from the mundane—not feeling well, headaches, fatigue—through the serious—inability to hold a job—to the spectacular—daily vomiting of glow-in-the-dark vomit, ejaculation of semen that scalds anyone who comes in contact with it, diarrhea that caused a spinal condition that confines a veteran to a wheelchair.

All in all, it's a syndrome that, at best, will be difficult to investigate because of the myriad exposures and symptoms. More likely, it is a collection of physical and psychosomatic illnesses that occur, or can be imagined, in any population of sufficient size.

The federal government assembled a panel to investigate Gulf War syndrome. The panel's November 1996 report concluded there was no evidence that any particular illness was associated with Gulf War service.

The Gulf War veteran population had diseases at the same (or lower) rates than would be expected in any population of that age and size. The more spectacular symptoms didn't stand up to serious examination.

President Clinton thanked the panel for its work. Then he announced the panel's report wasn't final, that the panel would be kept on, with some membership changes, and that the panel's budget would be doubled to investigate the syndrome. What's that mean?

Apparently, the scientists didn't deliver the "right" answer to the president. Apparently he knows the answer about Gulf War syndrome, and the panel didn't get it. In other words, the war on behalf of the "official science" of Gulf War syndrome is not over yet.

Consensus science

"Consensus science" is a new phenomenon. It's billed as a way to assess the "prevailing" scientific view, to learn what "most" scientists think, to define "generally accepted" science.

But how do you get consensus science? Is there an election? A poll? No. It's much easier than that.

Consider the global warming debate, the most notable success of consensus science to date.

In 1996, the United Nations Intergovernmental Panel on Climate Change (IPCC) released its report on climate change. The report's summary contained the conclusion that " . . . the balance of evidence suggests a discernible [human] influence on climate."

More than 2,000 scientists from a variety of disciplines participated in developing the report. The participants included some who are hot on the global warming theory, some who are cool to the idea, and some who are lukewarm.

Not all the 2,000 were climatologists; most of them weren't. Not all 2,000 took part in drafting the report's executive summary. Nor did all 2,000 agree on the conclusions that appeared in the summary. The lesson for you is that 2,000 is a big number.

Advocates of global warming promote the 2,000 scientists as representing a scientific consensus that there IS such a thing as human-influenced global warming. You get the point. Line up some experts on your side and say they represent all experts.

Junk science

Junk science is exaggerated or overinterpreted science used to advance some predetermined, often politically correct, politically desired, or financially lucrative conclusion.

In the best light, junk science is poor science; in the worst light, it is fraud.

In 1996, Tulane University researchers published a study on the controversial topic of "environmental estrogens," also known as "endocrine disrupters."

Environmental estrogens are manmade chemicals found in our environment, food, and water that chem ically resemble human estrogen hormones. It has been theorized that environmental estrogens disrupt normal hormonal processes to cause everything from infertility to cancer to attention deficit disorder.

The Tulane results set off new alarms about low levels of pesticides in the environment. Whereas pesticides, when tested one at a time, produced innocuous estrogenic effects, exposure to two such pesticides was reportedly 150 to 1,500 times more potent. Quite a startling and potentially important finding, if true. After all, it is quite likely that most people are exposed to multiple "environmental estrogens" every day.

Knowing the attention their results were going to attract, the Tulane scientists might have repeated their experiments. They might even have carried out the same experiments in a colleague's laboratory to be certain the results were correct. They chose otherwise. The Tulane scientists rushed into print.

Then in November 1996, less than five months after *Science* published the Tulane research, a newsletter reported that four laboratories had tried—and failed— to replicate the Tulane findings. The failure was not from lack of trying: 10 different tests were used in the attempts to repeat.

In January 1997, *Science* printed a letter from scientists at the U.S. National Institute of Environmental Health Sciences, Texas A&M University, and Duke University reporting that the Tulane results could not be replicated. The Tulane scientists tried to explain these failures to replicate their results by saying that special or different conditions existed in their laboratory. But this explanation holds no water.

One of the basic principles of science and the scientific method is that the results of scientific research must be replicable by other scientists in other laboratories. (Special "conditions" are the stuff of magic, not science.) Failure to replicate laboratory results is one reason science fads such as cold fusion have gone bust.

A month later, *Nature*, the highly regarded international science journal, published results from British researchers who also reported that they were unable to replicate the Tulane claims. In March, the Tulane research came under heavy attack at the annual Society for Toxicology meeting.

Four months later, in July 1997, the Tulane researchers threw in the lab towel. In a letter to *Science*, the chief of the Tulane laboratory admitted that neither his laboratory nor any other laboratory had been able to replicate his laboratory's extraordinary findings.

What caused the irreproducible results? Perhaps time will tell. Perhaps we will never know.

The important lesson—well known to Chicken Little—is that exciting claims about impending doom have a ready audience. To be sure, some claims will be shown to be bogus, but checking and testing take time, and, besides, hardly anyone pays attention to the retraction of a doom-sayer's story.

The precautionary principle

It's best to think of the precautionary principle as "pretend science." It assumes the existence of facts.

The precautionary principle is the basis for many of today's governmental regulatory programs, including those at the Environmental Protection Agency (EPA), the Food and Drug Administration (FDA), and the Occupational Safety and Health Administration (OSHA). The rationalization for the precautionary principle is "better safe than sorry." It has cut off scientific debate and eliminated science from public policy.

The estimated risks from chemicals or other substances in food, water, and air, regardless of the level of ballyhoo around them, are almost always so small that they are undetectable. Those risks are unmeasurable, and any reductions in risk, should they be obtained, will be unmeasurable as well.

Risk assessments, as done by the government, brush all the uncertainties under the laboratory rug. Risk assessments substitute "science policy choices" or "default assumptions" for scientific inquiry.

Default assumptions include these:

- If a near-lethal dose of a chemical increases cancer rates in rats, then it also increases cancer risk in humans exposed to doses thousands of times lower.
- If a high level of radiation exposure increases cancer rates, then any level of radiation exposure increases cancer risk.

- If one study contains information that associates a chemical with a health effect, but another study doesn't, the "negative" study is ignored or downplayed.

Default assumptions are as routine as the daily commute home. They are so routine that they are taken to represent actual scientific knowledge. You want to keep it that way.

While the assumptions well serve the regulatory agencies, they inhibit scientific research. Results that contradict an assumption are not weighed against other results; they are weighed against the assumption, which has no underlying proof. Put bluntly, how many results are necessary to displace an assumption that is blessed by a government agency? Whatever it is, it must be a *big* number.

Official science, consensus science, junk science, and the precautionary principle all give the appearance of science. But they aren't real science. Moreover, they can be destructive to science.

Accepted as "good enough for policy," they make it difficult for scientists to obtain funding for research that might reveal them to be erroneous and to obtain fair hearings for results that contradict them.

Anyway, when contradictory science comes along, you can say the old assumptions "have stood the test of time." Leave it up to your opponents to explain that "standing the test of time" means only that the products of science substitutes have never been tested by real science.

CHAPTER 4
A Cautionary Note

Remember how Batman and Robin always escaped from the slow, agonizing death planned by the Joker, the Penguin, and the other archvillains in the *Batman* television series?

The bad guys always left the room after they thought there was no escape for the Dynamic Duo. And the Caped Crusader and Boy Wonder always had a trick up their sleeves to save their hides in the nick of time.

What's the lesson? Tune in tomorrow to find out. Same bat time. Same bat channel. (Just kidding!)

If you want to silence science, you have to be sure you finish the job. You must watch science get buzz-sawed.

President Clinton thought he could stop work on human cloning. He had an ethical argument. He had the FDA assert regulatory authority. Senators and representatives introduced legislation that would make it illegal.

But cloning escaped. A combination of biotechnology firms and scientific organizations opposed the proposed bill—and they won. That's one problem with efforts to silence science. Sometimes (rarely), the scientists will fight back.

And you have to be careful with consensus science. It can backfire. For years, promoters of environmental fears have been able to count on the National Research Council (NRC), a part of the National Academy of Sciences. While the NRC was generally skeptical about such fears, it left the door open to new information that might swing it to the side of doom and gloom. And that possibility is all you need to keep fears alive and the precautionary principle in play.

But 1996 was a bad year for those that counted on the NRC. One NRC report said that carcinogens—both natural and synthetic—in the human diet aren't worth worrying about, and that there are plenty of anti-carcinogens—again, both natural and synthetic—in our food.

Another NRC report basically ended the controversy over whether power lines cause cancer. The NRC said the evidence wasn't convincing in spite of diligent efforts to find a link.

It's embarrassing enough to have a group of scientists review the information and conclude that there's no real support for your pet idea. It's worse when a single experiment shows your idea is flat-out wrong. It's far worse when one of the experimenters is still in grade school.

Some 100,000 people worldwide are reported to have been trained in "therapeutic touch," a method for treating many maladies by manipulating a "human energy field" that surrounds individuals. In early 1998, a team of researchers, including a fourth-grade girl, reported in the *Journal of the American Medical Association* that trained practitioners of therapeutic touch were unable to detect any "energy field." And, unable to detect it, how could they manipulate it?

While that report doesn't spell the end for therapeutic touch, it certainly destroyed the technique's credibility for most people.

So you can't simply tie science to the train tracks and walk away. Science is even more resourceful than Batman. And science has a major ally. After years of your best efforts, the American public still likes science and has high hopes for it.

CHAPTER 5
A Final Word

As Paul Simon (of Simon and Garfunkel, not the former senator often portrayed by Al Franken) might put it, there must be 50 ways to silence science.

You can try banning research and education, cutting research funding, intimidating and harassing scientists, refusing to release data, preventing publication of results, discrediting scientists because of their funding sources, or building layers of official and consensus science to position the skeptical scientist as just another flaky outsider trying to crash the scientific family reunion.

But this "silencing" is much more than an academic concern. Because we—all of us—are robbed of the benefits of true science.

For instance, health care choices have been taken away from women. Lawsuits that falsely charged it had caused birth defects drove Bendectin, the only morning sickness drug ever available in the United States, off the market. Silicone breast implants are available only for breast cancer survivors who take part in FDA-approved studies.

Thanks in part to the anti-science approach to radiation, the prospect of safe, clean, and inexpensive electricity generated by nuclear power grows dimmer each year. We are bugged about using pesticides, but their reduced use will increase food costs. Costs are important. The National Cancer Institute urges everyone to eat five fresh fruits and vegetables daily to protect against cancer. More people will do it if fruits and vegetables are inexpensive.

The world's people have already paid a big price thanks to the pesticide panic. Just before the U.S. ban on DDT, the National Academy of Sciences concluded that use of the pesticide had saved as many as 500 million lives in two decades. Today, without DDT, more than 2 million die every year from malaria spread by mosquitoes.

To be sure, there are alternative pesticides, but they are too expensive for many countries, and they have toxicity problems of their own. A conspiracy between the Audubon Society and the Environmental Defense Fund silenced scientists who might have argued against the faulty science employed by those organizations.

Today we stand to wreak untold havoc on our economy, our health, and our future by suppressing science, whether in the global warming debate or other areas of controversy.

Some think it was the lead in cooking and eating utensils that caused the downfall of the Roman Empire. Today there are those who think that lead, along with global warming and synthetic chemicals in food, water, and air, and other things will cause our own downfall. Unfortunately, they might be right.

Not because global warming will cause epidemics of infectious disease. Or because man-made chemicals will cause epidemics of cancer or increased levels of infertility.

Rather, it is our rejection of scientific thinking and the suppression of scientific debate in these and other areas that could lead to our ultimate downfall, if not by the year 2000, then not long after.

Science and scientists are being silenced because global warming and synthetic chemicals and lead are such big risks that, we are told, we can't wait for research. We can't delay action. But acting on unfinished research and incomplete evidence would be the ultimate triumph of those who would silence science today.

It may be hard to see exactly how science will survive the current onslaught. But it surely will. The truth will out. But the questions remain: Why, in the meantime, should anyone be denied the many benefits of truth? Why should anyone be made to suffer because we have silenced science?

ABOUT THE AUTHORS

Steven J. Milloy, the publisher of the Junk Science Home Page (http://www.junkscience.com), is the author of *Science without Sense: The Risky Business of Public Health Research* (Cato Institute, 1995), *Choices in Risk Assessment: The Role of Science Policy in the Environmental Risk Management Process* (Regulatory Impact Analysis Project, 1994), and *Science-Based Risk Assessment: A Piece of the Superfund Puzzle* (National Environmental Policy Institute, 1995). A lawyer, he first trained in the natural sciences, then specialized in health sciences and biostatistics.

Michael Gough is the director of science and risk studies at the Cato Institute. He is the author of *Dioxin, Agent Orange* (Plenum, 1986); co-editor of *Readings in Risk* (with T. S. Glickman, Johns Hopkins University Press, 1990); and author of more than 40 papers about environmental and occupational health as well as numerous newspaper op-eds. Gough, a Ph.D., is a biologist by training and a former staff member at two universities as well as at the National Institutes of Health and the congressional Office of Technology Assessment.

CATO INSTITUTE

Founded in 1997, the Cato Institute is a public policy research foundation dedicated to broadening the
parameters of policy debate to allow consideration
of more options that are consistent with the tradi-
tional American principles of limited government,
individual liberty, and peace. To that end, the
Institute strives to achieve greater involvement of
the intelligent, concerned lay public in questions of
policy and the proper role of government.

The Institute is named for *Cato's Letters*, libertarian
pamphlets that were widely read in the American
Colonies in the early 18th century and played a
major role in laying the philosophical foundation for
the American Revolution.

Despite the achievement of the nation's Founders,
today virtually no aspect of life is free from government encroachment. A pervasive intolerance for
individual rights is shown by government's arbitrary
intrusions into private economic transactions and its
disregard for civil liberties.

To counter that trend, the Cato Institute undertakes
an extensive publications program that addresses the
complete spectrum of policy issues. Books, mono-
graphs, and shorter studies are commissioned to
examine the federal budget, Social Security, regulation, military spending, international trade, and myriad other issues. Major policy conferences are held
throughout the year, from which papers are published thrice yearly in the *Cato Journal*. The
Institute also publishes the quarterly magazine
Regulation. In order to maintain its independence, the
Cato Institute accepts no government funding. Contri-

butions are received from foundations, corporations, and individuals, and other revenue is generated from the sale of publications. The Institute is a nonprofit, tax-exempt, educational foundation under Section 501(c)3 of the Internal Revenue Code.

CATO INSTITUTE
1000 Massachusetts Avenue, N.W.
Washington, D.C. 20001